THE VIRGIN PEN

A GUIDE TO WRITING YOUR 1ST BOOK WITH CONFIDENCE

ANTOINETTE BEEKS

> *"Buried in the cemetery are dreams that were never fulfilled, books that were never written, ideas that never became reality, visions that never manifested..."*

DR. MYLES MUNROE

This book is dedicated to Mary. I extend my heartfelt appreciation for keeping me accountable. I am eternally grateful.

CONTENTS

Introduction   ix

PART ONE
MINDSET

1. Who I Think I Am   3
2. Empower Your Pen   13

PART TWO
SETUP FOR SUCCESS

3. Craft a Blueprint for Success   23

PART THREE
NAVIGATING THE WRITING & EDITING JOURNEY

4. Nurture Your Writing   37
5. Embrace the Art of Editing   47

PART FOUR
THE NEXT STEP

6. Your Next Chapter   55

About the Author   59
Appendix   61
References   65

INTRODUCTION

Dear Author,

I want you to know that someone out there needs to hear your story. It is this very reason which compelled me to write *The Virgin Pen: A Guide to Writing Your 1st Book With Confidence.*

My mission is to equip you with the necessary tools to overcome the challenges of doubt, fear, and procrastination that may be holding you back from writing your first book. I understand what it's like to have a story burning inside you, yet being unsure of where to start or what to say due to the constraints we place on ourselves. I've wondered if anyone would even want to hear my message. These thoughts can be paralyzing for a new writer. However, I want you to know that whether it's been one year or 10 years since the idea of your book first entered your heart— it's never too late to start writing.

As I listened to my friends express their longing to write a book, I realized that I couldn't just be the friend they confided in. I had to take that glimmer in their eyes and run with it. I became determined to provide them with a nudge of encouragement, simple tools, and faith the size of a mustard seed.

I offer *The Virgin Pen* to guide you in taking your book from conception to completion. Believe in the power of your story, fellow writer! Someone out there is waiting to hear it. With my unwavering support and the resources provided in *The Virgin Pen*, you will find the confidence and guidance you need to bring your book to life. Your story matters: let's embark on this journey together.

Warm regards,

Antoinette

#thevirginpen

PART ONE
MINDSET

CHAPTER 1
WHO I THINK I AM

66 I alone cannot change the world, but I can cast a stone across the water to create many ripples."

MOTHER TERESA

WHO I THINK I AM

"Who do I think I am to write a book?" the antagonist whispered.

The enemy skillfully plants seeds of doubt using a first-person narrative to foster the illusion that negative thoughts are stemming from your psyche. Before writing my first book, I spent months listening to this negative voice questioning who I was to write a book. I had to overcome the reasons many authors quit before they start: lack of confidence, fear of failure or rejection, procrastination... Sound familiar?

As I pushed my way through the obstacles, I fostered compassion for new writers. Empathy led me to create this guide for those who desire to write but are experiencing doubt and hesitancy. God woke me up and gifted this assignment.

It was confirmed when, unexpectedly, several of my friends and associates started expressing their dreams to one day write their first book. I made a mental inventory of their brilliance and how much better the world would be if they put their story on paper. Unfortunately, overshadowing their hope was a familiar, dark cloud of doubt and hesitation looming on the horizon as they expressed their dream.

I heard their passion. I felt their struggle.

I know how it feels to have a story trapped inside. I would compare it to a warm soda on a scorching summer day: bubbling on the inside and ready to come out, but with no means to vent. It feels chaotic yet exhilarating.

Step out on faith using *The Virgin Pen* as your guide. Look back and have no regrets. Commemorate today as the day you committed to write (or finish) your first book. You're an author with a message. You're not an "aspiring author" or a "future author"—you are an author! Let that sink in.

The Virgin Pen: A Guide to Writing Your 1st Book with Confidence provides knowledge and insight from a fellow Author, a decade experienced quality assurance Editor, a believer in God, and a Wellness Coach.

Upon completing this guide, you will gain the tools to:

- Overcome mental hurdles associated with writing a book
- Enhance your writing skills
- Establish a straightforward and effective writing routine

Dare to answer, who do you think you are?

EMPOWER THE MIND

When undertaking a significant endeavor, feelings of inadequacy or self-doubt may emerge.

This can be overcome through action, positive thinking, and taking small steps. Break down larger tasks into more achievable goals. This can be done by entering your book's title and name on the first page or writing your first few sentences.

Conquer self-doubt by studying your topic, keeping the reader's best interest in mind, and having faith in your message. The Bible declares you to be more than a conqueror. Not only are you equipped to write a book, but you're equipped to promote it, to speak passionately about it, to generate income from it, to inspire others, and to pen even more books.

Recap:

- Have faith in you and your message
- Study your topic
- Take small steps

HOW DO I OVERCOME PERFECTIONISM?

When something is imperfect, it is perfect—and vice versa.

The thought of all eyes fixated on my words made me vulnerable as a first-time writer. As an experienced editor, the thought of missing a typo made me cringe. Perfectionism, if unchecked, has the power to paralyze and stifle your creative spirit.

Even during the creation of this book, the falsehood of perfectionism lingered in the back of my mind. I understood the importance of trusting my abilities and the tools I had. I just started writing, simple as that. Once the words started to flow, my focus shifted from perfectionism to progress. I became excited about the genius within.

Recap:

- Success comes through progress
- Editing tools will catch the majority of errors
- Reframe perfection

WHAT QUALIFIES ME TO WRITE A BOOK?

Life inherently shapes us into subject matter experts (or SMEs).

Whether it's mastering plumbing systems, closing deals, grooming pets, styling hair, designing clothes, leading a team, or cooking delectable pies, there are areas where our proficiency shines. These are the things we execute flawlessly, repetitively, and more efficiently than others in similar positions. Recognizing your own exceptionalities is key; everyone has a "thing" they excel at.

Discovering innovative solutions to existing problems solidifies your expertise to write a book. The strategies I developed to improve my health and lose weight without sacrificing delicious food (a feat many find difficult) unknowingly became the premise of my first book. This motivated me to pursue certification in wellness coaching and to write *After the Nest: The Culinary Edition.*'

Consider enhancing your credibility by seeking certifications or additional training in the topic you want to write about. Seminars and courses provide a knowledge boost and enhance credibility on your book topic. This not only elevates your expertise but also instills confidence when talking about your book.

Recap:

- Life shapes expertise
- Identify proficiency
- Boost credibility

HOW TO IGNORE NEGATIVE OPINIONS

I wanted to title this section "When Expecting a Red Carpet," but I digressed.

After breaking the news of my writing adventure to someone I love, I awaited a *"That's awesome! Go for it, Nette!"*

or a high-five response. Instead, I was greeted with a turned-up face and a disparaging question: "*Has that ever been done before?*" The glowing enthusiasm held moments before was swiftly dimmed by a burgeoning hurt.

I can laugh about it now, but in the moment it stung like lingering pepper spray after a nightclub brawl. Once I scooped up my feelings, emotional intelligence kicked in. I researched to determine if my book topic had already been published. After a two-day deep dive, my findings yielded the following: **irrelevant.**

Whether your topic has been published holds no significance. Your vision and how you convey an idea belongs solely to you. Yes, there may be thousands of books on fixing a crankshaft, but there will only be one book about how YOU fix a crankshaft. Your content stems from your wisdom and unique perspective. This is why God instilled the vision in you: to believe, conceive, and manifest it.

Recap:

- Own your vision
- Embrace resilience
- Focus on conveying your unique perspective

WHAT IF NO ONE WANTS TO BUY MY BOOK?

I still find it hard to believe that questioning my book's marketability was once a challenge for me.

It's common for doubt to surface right before undertaking something major; subconscious responses arise to hold us in a comfortable state. When this occurs, it's an indication to move forward. I had to become confident in knowing that I had something valuable to offer. Having trust in your gift is crucial.

Perhaps your book won't be a bestseller, but perhaps it will. Whether you sell 100 copies or 100,000 copies, take time to celebrate the commitment and diligence it takes to write a book. Acknowledge that your message can finally transition from your head and onto paper—no small feat! Be mindful that initial book sales may come from friends, family, and colleagues as your first group of supporters.

Looking back at my first book, I feel a sense of nostalgia. I'm amazed by the hard work and dedication that brought it to fruition, and I marvel at the brilliance it captures. Your book may undoubtedly evoke similar feelings.

Recap:

- Focus on your message instead of accolades
- Recognize limiting beliefs
- Believe your message will inspire, empower, transform

EXERCISE: "IDEAL BOOK VISION"

Challenge yourself to define your ideal book and list two key details of your observation.

_____

_____

_____

_____

_____

_____

_____

_____

_____

_____

_____

_____

_____

_____

_____

Formulate a strategy to achieve one of those ideals.

NOTES

CHAPTER 2
EMPOWER YOUR PEN

 Fate favors the brave."

CLIFFORD "T.I." HARRIS, JR.

EMPOWER YOUR PEN

Belief is where confidence begins.

When you think about having the confidence to write a book, what comes to mind? Do you believe that there's an exhaustive list of qualities you must possess? If so, take a moment to examine those beliefs.

Once you take inventory of your beliefs, writing your book becomes less scary and more attainable. It allows you to summon that once-formidable doubt monster from beneath the bed and confront it for what it truly represents: a fleeting emotion that can be replaced with a more supportive one. I needed a confidence catalyst to dissolve the fear of authoring my first book. Take a moment to examine the word confidence.

> Confidence (n): *faith* in one's *capabilities*
> to *overcome challenges* & achieve
> *success*

Pay careful attention to the key words in this definition, starting with *capabilities*.

CAPABILITIES

Ponder your superpower.

Are you creative, a critical thinker, a leader, a teacher, or a great communicator? Are you compassionate? When people compliment you, do they highlight certain skills? Identify which of your talents cause you to excel in life.

Identifying your capabilities and assessing how you show up can be used to overcome the challenge of writing a book.

CHALLENGES

Organizing and editing my book came easy to me, but it was consistency and accountability that were my biggest challenges.

What challenges come to mind when you think of writing your first book? Is it procrastination, perfectionism, or resources? Identifying and evaluating our challenges often reveals that they are smaller in reality than they appear in our thoughts. Once this is realized, you can determine action steps to overcome the challenge.

OVERCOME

Taking the necessary steps to overcome a challenge may feel awkward and daunting at first. Once I developed and placed my writing sessions on a visual calendar to look at daily, my dedication and consistency dramatically improved. Being held accountable forced me to act.

In all things that have purpose and meaning, an action on our part must occur. Embrace the feeling of overcoming— it will likely be the part of the journey you cherish the most.

SUCCESS

When you ponder the success of your book, what do you see? Is it personal fulfillment, prosperity, career advancement, recognition, or making a positive impact? Envision what you expect to happen with your book.

When I visualize success, I see 10,000+ women who confidently wrote their first book using *The Virgin Pen: A Guide to Writing Your 1st Book With Confidence*. I look deeper and envision each of these women impacting 10,000+ women using their book. Do you see how I illustrated my vision in the past tense? This is *"the assurance of things hoped for, the conviction of things not seen."*

FAITH

See the end results in the beginning.

Visualization is the secret weapon of manifestation. It involves trusting all of your senses. Be a kid again—envision your finished book in hand. Let your imagination run wild.

Visualize the colors of your cover. Are they vibrant? What does the texture of the cover feel like? Is it smooth and glossy, or is it a matte finish that's rough to the touch? Observe the scent of the pages. Etch this image into the canvas of your mind, store it in the album of your heart, and make it a piece in the gallery of your soul. See the end in the beginning.

If you don't believe in your vision and purpose, why would the reader?

Recap:

- Recognize and evaluate challenges
- Identify your unique superpowers
- Use visualization for manifestation

WRITING WITH PURPOSE

To build confidence in writing a book, it's crucial to understand the true essence of *why* you want to write a book.

Connecting to your book's purpose establishes an emotional bond that's likely to resonate with your readers. This connection anchors your focus and serves as a compass to guide your journey. Use your purpose to fuel perseverance.

In my first book, finding my voice was initially challenging. However, upon stepping back, I realized that writing is comparable to having a conversation. This realization prompted me to recalibrate and understand (1) who I was writing the book for and (2) why my message was so important.

Before going deep into finding the true purpose of my first book, I assumed my 'why' was to help young graduates become their own chef, save money, and stay sexy. When I dove deeper, I realized my 'why' was their overall well-being. I held tightly to that focus as I penned *'After the Nest: The Culinary Edition'*.

In a similar fashion, before writing *The Virgin Pen*, I had an image of a woman with a secret dream locked away in her heart. I watched her story unfold as the star of her own movie, and I imagined her motivations, joys, irritations, dreams, and challenges. She longed to write her first book but lacked the confidence, resources, and tools. Her hope dimmed each day she delayed in fulfilling her dream to write a book.

MY 'WHY' FOR THE VIRGIN PEN

Understanding your reader's character is crucial. Identifying their needs, envisioning how your book will transform them, and recognizing why they need your message shapes the content. Instead of a "target market," consider a "magnet audience" who will be drawn in to benefit from your content. Knowing your audience's lifestyle and challenges as they relate to your topic allows you to write for their needs.

Recognizing their challenges and goals provides insight into how your book can innovate. Whether offering an escape from reality, enhancing expertise, increasing awareness, or providing revelation, your book becomes a transformative experience for both you and the reader.

Recap:

- Find your voice
- Build confidence through purpose
- Envision transformation

EXERCISE: "IDEAL BOOK VISION"

Challenge yourself to define your ideal book and list two
key details of your observation.

_____

_____

_____

_____

_____

_____

_____

_____

_____

_____

_____

_____

_____

_____

_____

Formulate a strategy to achieve one of those ideals.

NOTES

PART TWO
SETUP FOR SUCCESS

CHAPTER 3
CRAFT A BLUEPRINT FOR SUCCESS

> " Until I put forth the time, resource, and effort, it will continue to be a goal on my vision board."

DARLENE HAGOOD

CRAFT A BLUEPRINT FOR SUCCESS

Writing a book was a new endeavor for me.

Going into it, I thought I could just sit and write, and a book would magically appear.

No.

Not establishing a strategy ahead of time led to sporadic writing when time permitted, or when I felt like it. I soon realized I was putting my book last in everything that was going on in my life.

I needed a plan to focus my time and energy in the right direction, a plan to tell me what to do and when to do it, and a plan to get my body and spirit aligned. I knew that once that plan was laid out, the "how" would come.

To start, I began collecting my intellectual property—aka notes.

THE COLLECTION PHASE: GATHER YOUR SCATTERED NOTES AND DATA

I'm willing to bet that when the concept hit you to write a book, you started radiating all sorts of wonderful ideas!

As soon as a concept hit me, I expeditiously started jotting. Ideas came at the most peculiar times. I had no choice but to use whatever was at hand to capture my thoughts: post-it-notes, scraps of paper, emails and text messages I had sent to myself... Ideas were stashed in my car, coat pockets, phone, laptop, kitchen drawers, journals, work desk, notebooks, everywhere.

If this is you, take a day or so to collect and compile your intel into one location. Doing this instantly brought me relief just by knowing my ideas were accounted for. I was stoked! After the collection phase, I organized my content.

CREATE A LIST OF POINTS

This step is crucial in the process—very crucial.

Create a list of points to discuss in each section and the order they will be presented. Use this list as a roadmap for providing guidance on what to focus on during each writing interval. Without it, you'll find yourself adrift and lacking direction. Learn from my experience. Otherwise, you may reach the conclusion of your book only to discover that your presentation is inconsistent, and your ideas are scattered without cohesion.

Utilizing a list promotes a seamless flow from cover to cover, sparing you the need to rearrange or rewrite information during the editing process. The cool part is that the list of points you have can turn into your chapter names, which becomes your table of contents.

THE TABLE OF CONTENTS

The first thing I do when I open a book is peruse the list of chapters (also known as the table of contents). Its purpose is to provide a glimpse into the book's content and capture the reader's interest. In your list, assign each point a 3-to-5 word description or title. Keep in mind that having a list of contents is not applicable to or necessary for all books.

Your outline doesn't have to be perfect, so don't worry about getting it right the first time. It may change, so be flexible. For now, call each chapter "Chapter X." This naming convention proves beneficial when rearranging your list, as you can finalize the chapter names and page numbers when you finalize the book.

Recap:

- Centralize your data
- Outline key elements
- Create a flow

ESTABLISH A SOLID WRITING PLAN

Breaking the big goal down into bite-size, digestible pieces was the turning point for me. Once I laid out the details, my mind was free to focus on writing. Doing this made life so much easier and kept me from feeling overwhelmed.

On a sheet of paper, I brainstormed everything I could do to write my book from cover to cover. (Sidenote: This list also included things I could do if I wanted to suck).

On this sheet of paper, I created a checklist that features the following:

- Goal
- Purpose
- Days to write
- Times to write
- Date to start
- Dates to complete each section
- Dates to celebrate
- Dates to edit
- Date by which to have the book done

A CHECKLIST FOR SUCCESS

To conquer major projects, I rely heavily on checklists. Checklists tell me the small tasks that need to be completed in order to achieve the big goal. Doing this relieves me of having to rely on memory, especially when dealing with the other responsibilities of life. It instructs me on what needs to be done and when, and it holds me accountable.

To develop your writing strategy, access *The Virgin Pen Companion: A Checklist for Success* in the appendix. It helps prioritize your writing project by breaking down the overall goal into smaller tasks. Use this checklist to monitor your progress so you can celebrate your accomplishments and milestones along the way.

ESTABLISH A SUITABLE WRITING SCHEDULE

Time management poses one of the most significant challenges when it comes to completing a book.

At first, I approached writing with an aloof attitude, allowing less significant matters to take precedence. However, the right time never comes; you have to create it. In the midst of balancing life, plug writing time into your daily activities. It's imperative to ensure external demands do not encroach on writing your book.

Analyze your natural rhythms. If you're an early bird, writing first thing in the morning may be optimal. Carve out time in the A.M. For night owls, consider writing during the nighttime hours. Aligning with the time of day when your creativity is at its peak proves effective.

Next, decide on which days and at which times you will write. I've discovered that sticking to the same time for each writing session fosters consistency. Once you've established your writing schedule, add it to your calendars and set alarms. Make sure to integrate breaks into your schedule to avoid burnout. Weaving together the responsibilities of life and authoring involves a well-thought-out plan.

Determination is the cornerstone; planning is the foundation.

DEFINE YOUR WRITING GOALS

Once you've created the writing schedule, set clear and measurable goals.

This involves establishing a goal for word count or writing duration. It also involves identifying milestones to reach within a defined time.

A **word count goal** allows you to specify the exact number of words you plan to write in any given session. This could be 500 to 1,000 words (or one to two pages), or any number that aligns with your overall writing goals.

If you thrive in high-pressure situations, consider opting for a **writing duration goal**. This allows you to allocate a specific amount of time with a definitive start and end. This could be 30 to 60 minutes, depending on your writing goal, but make sure to use a timer to manage your writing session. Using the duration goal method proved effective for me because it increased my focus as I operated within a limited amount of time. Creating time blocks also helps in letting others know your availability, thus reducing interruptions. This makes it easier to stay focused, whether you're working alone or with your family.

A **milestone goal** represents a significant point in your writing progress, such as completing a specific chapter or section in your book. Establishing milestone goals allows you to identify accomplishments as you progress in your writing.

ESTABLISH A REWARDS SYSTEM

Add celebration to your writing schedule.

As you build your strategy, remember to incorporate celebrating your success. This prompts you to take a moment to celebrate as you hit achievements like reaching your word count goal or completing a chapter.

Celebrating milestones has been found to trigger the release of dopamine, a neurotransmitter associated with pleasure and reward, thus contributing to feelings of happiness and motivation. If you really think about it, a rewards system can genuinely motivate you to get things done. That's a win-win.

Treat yourself to something special, whether it's a meal at your favorite restaurant, a relaxing candlelit bubble bath, or a spontaneous day trip. It's the small goals that achieve the big vision.

Once you establish the plan, seek reinforcement to execute it.

THRIVING TOGETHER: THE ROLE OF AN ACCOUNTABILITY PARTNER

This requires bringing out the big guns.

Imagine how much farther you could go if you had someone pushing you into greatness—someone to hold you accountable to doing what you said you were going to do. Let me give you a little background on how my first book came to be.

I asked a longtime friend and published author to hold me accountable in writing my first book. Little did I know she was going to take her assignment seriously. Very seriously. I recall the days of dodging her calls. When I finally kept our lunch meeting, her opening statement with the straightest face was "Where are my pages?" No "Hello Antoinette, how are you?" She wanted answers as to where the pages of my book were that I pledged to write by our next meeting. She was ruthless and didn't care about my feelings. I ducked and dodged for weeks, until I finally put on my big-girl panties and got to work. I am forever grateful for her push.

When you choose an accountability partner, pick someone who will hold you to your writing goals. This person could be a fellow writer, friend, family member, or mentor— someone you trust and who understands your writing aspirations. Choose someone that cares more about your destiny than your feelings. Choose someone that will keep you on your toes, then decide effective ways to maintain open communication with them.

ESTABLISH YOUR WRITING SPACE

Now that you have someone lighting a fire upon thine butt, designate your writing space.

Your environment plays a significant role in the success of your book. Create a space that promotes inspiration, productivity, and creativity. Have within eyeshot positive affirmations that will keep you motivated.

Details of lighting and temperature of the space may seem insignificant, but they have a tremendous impact on your end product, so adjust accordingly. If you desire background noise, consider writing in a coffee shop or listening to white noise. If you thrive in a silence, find a quiet area. If you live in a busy area where noise is inevitable, try using comfortable earplugs or headphones that drown out noise, or consider reserving a room at your local library.

Ensure your writing tools are easily accessible (writing device, chargers, writing stylus or pen, a place to jot notes, highlighters) to minimize breaks in your concentration as you write.

Recap:

- Have a plan
- Celebrate big and small wins
- Set yourself up for success

EXERCISE: "CRAFTING YOUR WRITING PLAN"

Use *The Virgin Pen Companion: A Checklist for Success* to develop a writing plan by defining goals, breaking down tasks, and setting deadlines.

_____

_____

_____

_____

_____

_____

_____

_____

_____

_____

_____

_____

_____

_____

_____

Review and adjust regularly to achieve your goals.

NOTES

PART THREE
NAVIGATING THE WRITING & EDITING JOURNEY

CHAPTER 4
NURTURE YOUR WRITING

The creation of a thousand forests is in one acorn."

RALPH WALDO EMERSON

NURTURE YOUR WRITING

While a few people have managed to write entire books in one go, it's unlikely to happen on your first try.

Initially, your thoughts may seem chaotic and lack structure. You might question if they even make sense. However, chaos often precedes a masterpiece. Similar to an artist with a half-complete canvas, trust that your vision will be cohesive in the end.

When contemplating how to begin, start with the first topic on your list of contents. Envision your words flowing effortlessly like a river. Maintain focus on the words you do have and believe that the words you don't have will come eventually.

STAY STRONG AND OVERCOME TEMPTATION

I remember the moments when I would be getting ready for a writing session. Without fail, my phone would chime with invites from friends to hang out. It was as if the enemy knew the exact time of my session. I reasoned that if there was such a strong effort to distract me, there must be something within my book that the adversary was attempting to conceal from the world. This made me dig deeper into efforts to protect my time. You must do the same.

Overcome idle social media scrolling and incessant binge watching as you write your book. You don't want to look back a year from now and regret losing valuable time.

If possible, silence non-emergency notifications on your phone. I find utilizing the 'Do Not Disturb' feature or activating airplane mode is helpful in minimizing distractions. To further reduce interruptions and the temptation of idle scrolling, place your phone in a separate room and rely on your computer as your timer and tool to conduct any necessary research.

Talk to your family, friends, or the people in your household to get their buy-in to support you in your writing journey. Communicate your writing schedule and request that they give you solitude and quiet during that time. If your friends are accustomed to spending time with you, lovingly let them know ahead of time that you're on an important assignment.

HURDLE THE WRITER'S BLOCK

There may be times in your writing process where you experience a loss of words. You may stare at the screen with your hands resting patiently on the keys, waiting for something to hit you. Don't fret; your knowledge well hasn't run dry. What you are experiencing is called writer's block. Your creative flow may halt, or you might struggle to articulate even the simplest of sentences. This can happen at any moment and to any author.

The key is to be aware of writer's block. It may be an indicator that your mind needs to shift to something else momentarily in order to recalibrate. If you're struggling to expound on a specific idea, don't stress too much about finding the perfect words. Instead, jot down the idea or thought, and come back to it when you feel inspired to expand on it further.

Taking a break, getting rest, spending time in nature, and journaling helped me hurdle writer's block. Whatever you do, **DO NOT LINGER** in this place. Take a deep breath and move forward.

EDIT LATER

Resist the temptation to correct typos while you write.

As a perfectionist, I've experienced the inclination to perfect every detail as I type. I eventually realized that this was impeding my thought process and interrupting my pace. I learned to let go and just write.

Engaging in editing while in the midst of writing can also stifle creativity. When crafting your initial draft, concentrate only on transferring your thoughts to the page. The opportunity to refine and polish your work will come later. Keep in mind: Your first draft doesn't need to be flawless.

DO ONE THING AT A TIME

While it's tempting to explore every beautiful idea, remember that staying true to your original writing intent enhances the impact of your session. Focus on the core of your narrative and let your creativity shine within that framework.

Unless your instincts strongly guide you to shift focus, consider gently setting aside any new ideas to explore later. Stay committed to your established writing goal for the session; this not only maintains focus but also minimizes the chance of becoming overwhelmed. When a brilliant idea arises, capture it by jotting it down. Then, smoothly return to your original thought process. Fleeting thoughts are a natural part of the creative journey. Acknowledge them, appreciate the spark, and confidently move forward with your narrative.

STAY MOTIVATED

During the initial stages of writing your book, you may feel motivated, on cloud nine, and prepared for any challenge. However, as time progresses, that initial enthusiasm may wane. Doubts and second-guessing might creep in, causing you to question your initial motivation or contemplate quitting. You might even find yourself on a prolonged hiatus from when you first began.

It's essential to recognize that these experiences are entirely normal. I'm sure there are many authors who can attest to having experienced these emotions at some point in their writing journey. Remember, you are not alone in facing these challenges.

I discovered that taking it one day at a time was incredibly helpful. Being present in the moment and concentrating on a single thought kept me motivated during my writing sessions. I centered my focus on the reader's needs. The anticipation of being the first author in my family filled me with excitement, while the prospect of my work becoming an immortalized part of history further fueled my motivation.

The key is to confidently put one foot in front of the other and trust that your perseverance and dedication will yield success. Envision the completion of your book. Relish and savor the present moment, allow passion to take the wheel, and let the fuel of determination thrust you forward.

TIPS FOR WRITING WITH EASE

Have you ever been so engrossed in a book that you completely lost track of time while seamlessly being led from one chapter to the next?

I didn't realize at the time of writing my first book that I was applying a practice called literary transition. Depending on the nature of your book, you may be able to apply these techniques to your literary work.

Applying **foreshadowing** allows you to drop hints about what's to come in the next chapter or section. It builds anticipation and creates a sense of harmony within your narrative. It can be accomplished using a bridge sentence.

Bridge sentences act as connectors between chapters that guide the reader from one part of a book to the next. These sentences summarize key points from the previous section while introducing elements that will be explored in the upcoming chapter.

Depending on the nature of your book, consider using a moment of reflection at the end of each chapter. For example, you will see a "recap" at the end of various sections in this book. **Reflective transitions** serve as a synopsis of the chapter and give the reader an opportunity to take a natural pause. This way, they can reflect on the previous events before moving on to the next phase of the book.

Transitions play a significant role in maintaining flow and sustaining attention. Use transitions to keep your reader flowing from one part of your narrative to the next, thus keeping them wanting more of your story.

Now, what would be a good transition to discuss using automation to write?

USE AUTOMATION TO WRITE

When writing my book, there were moments when I didn't feel like typing.

I experimented with the dictation software installed on my computer. Speaking my thoughts, instead of typing them, gave my hands a break and helped incorporate a more casual, conversational feel into my book. Once I started using this dictation feature, I noticed how my personality began to shine through the words of my book.

Prior to utilizing dictation features, familiarize yourself with the respective software's verbal prompts. Mastering these prompts enables you to deliver precise commands, such as starting and ending sentences and applying punctuation. This proficiency saves time during editing by ensuring proper sentence structure from the outset.

ILLUSTRATE THE NARRATIVE

To add variety and interest, consider adding images or artwork to your book.

Visual imagery caters to visual learners and breaks up the monotony of reading text. Integrate relevant, high-resolution images near corresponding text to enhance reader engagement. Maintain a consistent style throughout the book, considering factors like color schemes and captions. Be mindful of copyright issues when using third-party images.

Recap:

- Create a team effort
- Take breaks when needed
- Use writing tools

EXERCISE: "VISUALIZATION TO STAY MOTIVATED"

Take a moment to think about completing your book and what it means to you.

_____

_____

_____

_____

_____

_____

_____

_____

_____

_____

_____

_____

_____

Visualize yourself achieving it and imagine how it will positively impact your life.

NOTES

CHAPTER 5
EMBRACE THE ART OF EDITING

Excellence is to do a common thing in an uncommon way."

BOOKER T. WASHINGTON

EMBRACE THE ART OF EDITING

In my dual role as both an editor and an author, I both appreciate the beauty and understand the importance and challenges associated with crafting a polished document.

Spelling, grammar, and punctuation errors have the potential to divert the reader's attention, causing them to overlook the core message in any media. It is crucial to invest time in performing at least three reviews while leveraging available tools to streamline your process.

REVIEW #1

This is the time to read your draft from beginning to end. This review is conducted to ensure your document is clear and flows naturally. If sentences are too long or wordy, consider breaking them up into multiple sentences. Conduct this review by reading your text aloud to spot any pacing issues. You may also consider using automation features that read your text aloud to you, as this allows you to listen for any inconsistencies in your writing.

Look for word variety. If you sense a particular word is being overused, use the word search function to count its frequency. While writing my debut book, I relied heavily on the term "satiate." Although essential for conveying my point, its excessive use swiftly became apparent and redundant, prompting the need for variety.

During the review of this book, I edited 116 usages of the word "can". Even though it's a simple word, its presence diminishes authority. If a particular word does not add value, consider removing or replacing it.

Use a thesaurus to replace redundant words. Unless you're trying to drive a point through reiteration, the overuse of a word can become verbose and boring for the reader. Varying your language adds depth to your message, making it fundamental for intellectual growth. Employing a thesaurus expands your vocabulary and gives the reader the opportunity to do the same.

Once you complete this review without needing to make any edits, reward yourself with a 24-hour break before moving on to the next review.

REVIEW #2

During this review, make corrections for spelling, grammar, and punctuation as you read the manuscript in its entirety. Utilize the spelling- and grammar-check tool on your device. While these tools may seem obvious, their application is often surprisingly overlooked. The spellcheck tool is your meticulous writing ally. It promptly identifies and offers corrections for grammar and punctuation errors, ensuring a polished, professional document. It streamlines editing, enhances efficiency, and elevates the overall quality of your writing. But be advised. With any automation tool, it is important to use critical thinking and judgment when it comes to employing such tools to ensure they don't misidentify mistakes or make incorrect suggestions.

REVIEW #3

Before proceeding with this review, consider taking a break. This break will allow you to approach the concluding review from a fresh perspective and with a rejuvenated focus. During this final evaluation, address any remaining issues to guarantee a thorough and accurate review.

OTHER EDITING TOOLS: ARTIFICIAL INTELLIGENCE (AI)

With the rise of technology, the use of artificial intelligence has become prevalent. AI has the capacity to automate editing and enhance sentence structure. If you opt to use AI, remember to always let your unique voice and creativity shine through your work. Trust your intuition when making your final edits; AI is a resource that should not be a substitute for human judgment, insight, or editing.

HIRE A PROFESSIONAL

Upon completing your self-reviews, consider hiring a professional editor for additional assessment. Independent evaluations play a vital role in adjusting layout and formatting, as well as uncovering errors that may have escaped your notice. Given that your perception of your writing may be biased, a professional proofreader offers an impartial perspective on your final draft. They can identify errors and offer valuable recommendations for improvement.

Recap:

- Use tools to ease the editing process
- Diversify your vocabulary
- Hire a pro to polish your work

EXERCISE: "UNCOVER THE HIDDEN TREASURES"

Discover the hidden gems in your writing. Look for moments of brilliance, clever wordplay, and beautifully crafted sentences that make your book shine.

_____

_____

_____

_____

_____

_____

_____

_____

_____

_____

_____

_____

_____

_____

_____

_____

_____

_____

NOTES

PART FOUR
THE NEXT STEP

CHAPTER 6
YOUR NEXT CHAPTER

> May He grant you your heart's desire, and fulfill your plans."

PSALM 20:4

YOUR NEXT CHAPTER

Celebrate!

Acknowledge the completion of your writing journey. Your Virgin Pen has conceived your baby and given life to your creation.

Technically, my work here is done, but I would be remiss if I didn't provide insight into the step that could catapult your life. That step is deciding if you want to keep your baby to yourself, or if you want to share it with the world.

If you decide to forge ahead and take the step into publication, keep in mind that you have two options. The first is the choice of going the traditional route and hiring a publisher to produce and distribute your book, while the second is going the independent route to self-publish your work.

Self-publishing has become a popular option since the inception of digital platforms and online distribution channels. For one, it allows authors to reach global audiences. There are also self-publication companies that can assist in the editing, formatting, cover design, branding, and marketing of your book.

However, before you hire a publication or branding company, be sure to do your research.

NAVIGATE THE PATH TO SUCCESSFUL PUBLICATION

Look for testimonials and reviews from other authors who have used the services you're considering. Take a moment to review the service provider's books, websites, and social media. If their content or online presence is low-quality or teeming with misspelled words, refrain from using them.

Ensure the service provider has successfully represented authors in your genre. For example, if you want to publish a cookbook, research providers that have experience and success in that arena.

Thoroughly review any contracts or agreements before committing to a service. Pay attention to terms related to royalties, rights, and any fees involved. Look for transparency and clarity in their terms. If you're unsure about any terms, consider seeking legal advice.

Congratulations on your endeavor!

Recap:

- Celebrate your accomplishments
- Consider publishing your book
- Do your publishing research

NOTES

ABOUT THE AUTHOR

Antoinette Beeks, a Greenville SC native, is the Amazon bestselling author of *After the Nest: The Culinary Edition*. She is also a chef, spiritual believer, expert pharmaceutical editor, and certified Wellness Coach. Her mission is to use this unique blend of knowledge to assert other women to reach their wellness goals, whether in health or writing their first book.

As a child, she was always intrigued by the fundamentals of the human body. This led her to pursue studies in Biology at Charleston Southern University. She went on to earn her Integrative Nutrition Health Coaching certification from the Institute for Integrative Nutrition. Working in the corporate arena, she had the opportunity to teach the employment sector tips for implementing wellness strategies, while maintaining demanding careers.

After crossing the paths of so many women who shared a desire to write their first book, God inspired her to write *The Virgin Pen: A Guide to Write Your 1st Book With Confidence*. Using the experiences and challenges of writing her first book, she developed *The Virgin Pen* as a nudge of encouragement for other women to follow their dreams to authorship.

Connect with Antoinette at
www.afterthenestllc.com

APPENDIX
THE VIRGIN PEN COMPANION:

A CHECKLIST FOR SUCCESS

THE VIRGIN PEN COMPANION:: A CHECKLIST FOR SUCCESS

Use this checklist to navigate your writing journey, monitor your progress, and celebrate your accomplishments along the way.

Instructions:

1. Enter the information into the fields.
2. Enter the target date to complete each task.
3. Select the checkbox when the task is complete.
4. Celebrate achieving milestones on the dates listed for the boxes containing an asterisk*.

The Virgin Pen Companion: A Checklist for Success

Goal of book	
Magnet audience	
Word count	_____ words per session
Writing duration	____:____ am pm **to** ____:____ am pm
Days to write (select)	☐ Mon ☐ Tues ☐ Wed ☐ Thurs ☐ Fri ☐ Sat ☐ Sun
Target completion date	
Accountability partner name	
Designate writing space	☐
Collect notes and data	☐
Create outline	☐
Establish milestone dates and rewards	☐

Task	Target Completion Date	✓
Table of contents		☐
Chapter 1		☐*
Chapter 2		☐
Chapter 3		☐
Chapter 4		☐*
Chapter 5		☐
Chapter 6		☐
Additional sections		☐
Review #1: Flow and content		☐
Review #2: Spelling, grammar, punctuation		☐*
Review #3: Address any remaining issues		☐
Hire professional editor		☐
Publish date		☐*

*Indicates milestone dates to celebrate progress and accomplishments.

REFERENCES

"The creation of a thousand forests is in one acorn."
Emerson, R. W. (1841). Essays: First Series. Boston: James Munroe and Company.

"Fate favors the brave."
@indapartmentspodcast @rydahsonly. (2023, August). [Fate Favors the Brave] Clifford "T.I." Harris, Jr. [Video]. YouTube. https://youtube.com/shorts/l59GUNGNNVI

"Now faith is the assurance of things hoped for, the conviction of things not seen."
Hebrews 11:1
New Revised Standard Version. (1989). Holy Bible New Revised Standard Version. Zondervan.

"May He grant you your heart's desire, and fulfill your plans."
Psalm 20:4
New Revised Standard Version. (1989). Holy Bible New Revised Standard Version. Zondervan.

"Until I put forth the time, resource, and effort, it will continue to be a goal on my vision board."
(2023, December 27). "Setting and Achieving Your Goals." A Dose of Inspiration (Darlene Hagood)